ANNA &

THE SNOW

GLOBE

A Child Overcoming Bullying

and Anxiety

By

Vicki Jones MBACP MSc BSc (Hons)

CHAPTER ONE

Anna ran across the playing fields, aware of the silence in the school grounds as she reached the path leading to the school gates. Although it was mid-December, she felt hot and uncomfortable in her dark grey and burgundy school uniform. Her blazer had slipped off her shoulders, and her thick black tights had a rip in one leg just below her left knee. Her light brown hair, which had been neatly brushed earlier that morning, was unkempt and hung down to her shoulders in a tousled mess.

Anna dreaded walking into the classroom as she knew full well she would be greeted by Miss Marmaduke's disapproving gaze and a telling off for being late three days in a row. The smug looks Anna knew she would receive from her classmates only added to her feelings of dread and humiliation. Anna's stomach churned at the thought of how her cousin, Sophie, would revel in her discomfort, and Anna could almost hear the conversation that would take place between her aunt and cousin later when she returned home.

Reaching the main entrance to the school, breathless and agitated, Anna pressed the buzzer for the receptionist to open the door. Despite the school being a cheery, one-storey building, with white rendered walls and climbing vines, set amid lush green fields and beautiful open countryside, Anna felt dismal gloom.

Feeling like she had been unhappy for a lifetime, Anna found it hard to believe it had only been nine months since her world had crumbled into pieces. In fact, Anna's world was so shattered and broken, she felt disconnected from the real world, as though she had been catapulted into a harsh and lonely place.

Focused on how she was feeling inside, Anna didn't spare a thought for her dishevelled appearance. The freshly painted classroom door was stuck when she tried to open it. After a mighty push, the door opened, and the force of Anna's thrust hurled her into the room so fiercely that she could barely control her balance. Struggling to regain her composure and her dignity, Anna became aware of the stifled giggles and the muffled reproachful comments from her classmates.

"It's good of you to pay us a visit, Anna," Miss Marmaduke uttered, between clenched teeth. "Third time late this week, and it's only Wednesday!" she added, sarcastically.

"She looks like she's forgotten how to dress properly and comb her hair," Anna's cousin, Sophie, sniggered.

The class, unable to contain their amusement any longer, emitted a loud roar of laughter.

"Quiet! Any more noise and you will all receive detention for one hour after school," a tight-lipped Miss Marmaduke snapped.

The classroom noise eventually subsided and Anna remained standing, red faced and feeling as if she were shrinking in size by the second. She felt dizzy and, for an awful moment, thought she might faint. Anna calmed herself down with the knowledge that she would not faint and the realisation that the symptoms she was experiencing, as unpleasant as they seemed, were merely the result of her body being full of tension.

Anna knew her brain's response, believing she had been in danger, was to flood her bloodstream with adrenaline in case she needed the extra strength to run or defend herself. This knowledge lessened the impact of any horrible thoughts Anna had about the possibility of fainting or never feeling normal again.

"It's known as the *'fight or flight'* syndrome," the nurse at Anna's doctor's surgery had once told her.

Anna reminded herself of the nurse's words: *the brain sends down the same signals to release adrenaline in case of physical and emotional danger. It's harmless, but it feels awful. Taking deep, relaxing breaths and relaxing your muscles will make the brain think that you're safe which will stop the adrenaline release, then no-one need know how you are feeling or even notice that you are relaxing your body.*

Doing as the nurse had told her, Anna composed herself as she made her way back to the third row of tables. She sat down and removed her English book from her school bag.

"Anna, I suggest you refer to your timetable. This is a *maths* lesson!" Miss Marmaduke hissed.

The class was in hysterics at Anna's situation once again. Amidst roars of laughter, the insults and retorts came across loud and clear. Cutting, deprecating comments made Anna feel as if she were shrinking into nothingness again.

"Such a loser!"

"What an idiot."

"Didn't her mother ever teach her how to dress?"

"How do you put up with her, Sophie?"

"Enough!" retorted Miss Marmaduke. "I want complete silence or there *will* be detention. For the rest of the lesson, with no more interruptions, please write down answers to exercise ten on page sixty-seven of your textbook. Thank you."

The bell rang for break. The sounds of books being flung into bags and the scraping of chairs as the children left their tables to make their way to the playground grated on Anna. She hated that sound because it was the precursor to either being ignored or tormented by Sophie and her spiteful friends. She wished there was somewhere to hide, but, unless it was raining, everyone had to go outside.

Anna slowly made her way to the playground. She wished she had some money so she could buy a packet of crisps to kill time, but the small amount of cash she was allowed only stretched as far as stationery for school and bus fares for when she wanted to go into town.

As Anna headed for the playground, she noticed Sophie, who was buying a drink and a snack from the canteen near the exit doors. Suddenly, without warning, Anna stumbled and almost fell to the ground as a blonde girl standing next to Sophie swiftly extended her leg in Anna's path as she walked towards the exit.

Ignoring the blonde girl and recovering her balance, Anna made her way to the playground, looking for anyone who appeared to be on their own. Fully aware of the other kids who were picked on, Anna would normally link up with them, but she had no such luck today. No-one she was friends with was around. In fact, lately Anna's friends were hardly ever around because they avoided school as much as they could.

Anna's heart seemed to dive into the pit of her stomach as she pondered on how dishevelled and sad she must look. In fact, it was hard to differentiate which was worse: how bleak and hopeless she was feeling or how vulnerable she must be looking. She empathised with how an antelope would feel upon spotting a tiger in the jungle, just waiting in dreaded anticipation for it to pounce at any moment.

To make matters worse, Anna saw Sophie and Sophie's two best friends, Amy and Laura, walking across the playground towards her. Amy, the blonde girl who had attempted to trip Anna up earlier, dropped a crisp packet and chocolate wrapper at Anna's feet.

"I should pick that up if I were you," mocked Sophie. "It's bad to drop litter."

"Oh, get lost, Sophie." Anna had learned it was easier to get angry at her cousin rather than show she was upset.

Laura shook her head in disbelief and asked Sophie, "How on *earth* do you put up with her at home?"

"With great difficulty," Sophie replied, as she glared at Anna with a look of contempt.

Before Anna could decide whether to retaliate or walk away, David, a boy in their class who had noticed what was going on, approached the four girls.

"Give it a rest, Sophie. You can be so horrible at times. You used to be nice, what's got into you?" asked David.

"It's not what's got into *me*, it's what's got into my house and into my school, that's what! It's *Anna*! I can't stand her. She wants attention all the time and when she doesn't get it, she plays the sad little loser. It's just an act, David. Ignore her," replied Sophie.

The conversation was interrupted by the bell signalling the children to return to class.

"You coming round after school?" Sophie asked David.

Sophie had known and secretly adored David since they were seven years old. Good looking, with blue-green eyes and wavy brown hair, he had an air of confidence about him. He was also captain of the football team and a good all-rounder in sports, making him popular with everyone.

David's reply astonished them all, but mostly Anna.

"Yeah, I'll be coming round, but to see Anna. If I come about six, Anna, do you fancy hanging out for a while, maybe coming to the park with Benjie and me?"

Benjie was David's cute terrier. Sophie had often accompanied them on their much loved walks in the small park near her house.

Anna was confused to the point where she felt almost stunned and could hardly reply. *Was he serious? Was he setting her up?* she wondered.

"Anna, is six okay?" he persisted

"Umm, yeah, yes, sure. See you at six."

Before the others, who were just as dumbfounded, had time to speak, Anna hurriedly made her way back to class. She could hardly believe it.

David, DAVID, of all people! Sophie will hit the roof. Is it worth it? Is it worth the fallout I will get from being friends with him? From a rational perspective, I guess it doesn't make much difference. Whatever I do will be wrong in Sophie's eyes. Also, David is just asking me to go for a walk, not to be his special friend, reasoned Anna.

After some thought, Anna was convinced she was overreacting and reassured herself that this wasn't a big deal.

However, as it happened, it *did* turn out to be a big deal.

Luckily, Sophie and her friends had swimming lessons in the lunch break, so Anna managed to avoid them for the rest of the day. When the bell rang at three thirty, Anna left the classroom as quickly as she could.

Arriving home before Sophie, Anna let herself in with her key and immediately made her way upstairs to her bedroom.

* * * * *

"It's not *fair*, Mum," wailed Sophie. She was sitting at the table in their newly fitted white kitchen and drinking a chocolate milkshake whilst complaining to her mother, who was preparing dinner.

"David is one of my best friends and now Anna's asked him to be *her* best friend."

"How do you know this?" asked Sophie's mother, in a steely voice.

"Because I was in the playground with Laura, Amy and David. Then Anna came and, ignoring me, asked David if she could walk Benjie with him later. As he didn't like to say no, he said he's coming round here at six to go with her to the park!" Sophie shrieked.

"The nerve of the girl!" exclaimed Sophie's mother. "Your father and I have been friends with David's parents since before you were born. What's got into David? I thought you both got on so well. Why on earth would he prefer Anna to *you*?"

"Well it's obvious isn't it?!" declared Sophie. "She's been telling lies about me. Amy said she heard Anna telling David how nasty I am and that I'm lazy in the house."

"*What!*" shrieked her mother. "We had the decency to take that girl in when she had nowhere else to go, and this is how she repays us? By talking about us and running us down. I dread to think what else she may be saying about us behind our backs! That girl is overstepping her mark. Don't worry, darling. I'll sort this out."

"I'll get her for you, Mum," volunteered Sophie, with a smug expression on her face.

* * * * * *

Anna was in her sparsely furnished room, hanging her school uniform on the back of the door, when Sophie burst in and demanded Anna go downstairs because Sophie's mother, Joan, wanted to speak to her.

"I wish you'd knock before you burst into my room, Sophie. You nearly sent me flying. I was behind the door!"

"Why should I knock in my own house?" retorted Sophie. "I've come to tell you that Mum wants you to go downstairs."

"I'll be down in a minute," sighed Anna.

"She wants you *NOW*," shouted Sophie.

"What does she want?" replied Anna.

"I have no idea. All I know is she's annoyed with you about something and she wants to see you downstairs *now*," Sophie demanded.

Anna sighed again. Wondering what on earth she had done this time to upset her aunt, she made her way downstairs and into the kitchen.

"Did you want me, Joan?"

Joan, who was removing a casserole dish from the oven, banged the dish down so hard on the work surface that Anna thought it was going to break.

"You wicked little madam!" screamed Joan. The words were spoken so venomously that Anna felt her stomach turn in a knot.

Joan continued her rant, "how *dare* you repay this family's kindness by turning Sophie's friends against us! If it wasn't for your uncle, I would have you out of this house and placed into care!"

Anna could feel the blood drain from her face. Her arms and legs felt weak, and she felt that horrible dizziness engulf her again. She felt sick, and for a moment she was terrified she may throw up in the kitchen.

"I... I don't know what you mean," Anna stammered. "I haven't said or done anything wrong."

"You tried to turn David against Sophie," her aunt retorted. "Our family has been friends with David's family for years, long before you came along! It makes me wonder what you will try to do next! You're nothing but a troublemaker. Get out of my sight. I don't even want to look at you!"

Anna ran out of the kitchen and upstairs to her room, fighting back tears. She opened the drawer of an old dressing table and brought out a photograph in a silver frame. Gazing with so much love at the photograph of her parents, who she desperately missed, Anna calmed herself down with the breathing and relaxation techniques the kind nurse had taught her.

Anna relaxed all of her muscles and breathed in slowly through her nose for three seconds, imagining she was blowing up a balloon in her belly. She then held her breath for a second before exhaling through her nose for just over three seconds and pretended she was deflating the imaginary balloon in her stomach. She waited two seconds and repeated the breathing technique ten times.

Anna knew the dizziness and the sick feeling were from stress. She knew it was important to relax her body and correct her breathing. After a couple of minutes, she began to feel better. She lay down on the bed, feeling more relaxed but exhausted. Anna had suffered similar attacks in the nine months since her parents were killed in a car crash.

However, living with Sophie and her mum, Joan, sometimes made it hard for Anna to relax during these attacks. Both Sophie and Joan were very hostile towards Anna, ever since Uncle Bill had brought her in to live with his family.

Anna was not sure if Bill knew the extent of Joan's and Sophie's resentment towards her as they were careful to hide it from him. Even so, Anna wondered if he suspected anything because she would often catch him gazing at her with such sadness in his eyes, although that could have been because she had lost her parents and he had lost his brother- and sister-in-law. Not wanting to make matters any worse than they were, Anna had decided not to tell Bill how she was treated. She hoped that, in time, Joan and Sophie would learn to at least like her, if not care for her.

Anna's thoughts were interrupted by the doorbell ringing. She heard her Aunt Joan open the door and greet David in a gushing tone.

"Hello David. How lovely to see you."

"Hello Mrs Johnson. Is Anna there? She said she would walk Benjie with me," David replied.

Anna sat up, hoping Joan would call her. Instead, she heard her aunt telling David that she had been in trouble at school earlier that morning for being late and wouldn't be going out.

"I'll call Sophie for you instead," she added, briskly. "Sophie! Sophie, darling! David is here!"

Anna shook her head in frustration and then heard Sophie leave her bedroom and walk down the stairs.

Sophie smiled, her eyes lighting up as she spoke. "Hi David. Hang on, I'll get my coat. Oh, you've got Benjie with you. We can take him to the park."

After hearing the front door shut, Anna looked out of her bedroom window and saw Sophie, David and Benjie walking together towards the park. Snowflakes had just begun to fall. Anna remembered being so happy the last time it had snowed. It had been last Christmas Eve; she and her mother had been so excited because it was going to be a white Christmas. Yet Anna was now feeling so sad and she couldn't imagine ever feeling happy again.

CHAPTER TWO

Leaving the house for school the next morning, the girls were dressed in rubber-soled walking boots, woollen hats and scarves. The snow had fallen so heavily overnight that it covered the ground like a soft white blanket. There was no grey to be seen as the pavements and rooftops were encrusted with fresh white snow, which glistened like diamonds touched by the rays of the sun. There was a rose-pink tinge to the sky, which made the scene even lovelier.

Again, Anna felt a wave of bittersweet nostalgia as she was reminded of this time last year, when a pink tinged sky had opened with white, fluffy snowflakes, making it the only white Christmas Anna could ever remember.

Laden with the bags Sophie made her carry for the school Christmas lunch, Anna's arms were already aching as the girls reached the front gate of the house. Anna spotted Sophie's two friends, Amy and Laura, walking towards them and also carrying bags of treats for the school party. Amy and Laura greeted Sophie and ignored Anna, which was nothing new.

It seemed that because Sophie hated Anna, everyone else had to join in. None of Sophie's friends had even given her a chance. They hadn't even bothered to get to know her. Apparently, Sophie's word was good enough. The girls had hardly passed the front gate when Joan came to the door and called for Anna to return to the house.

"Anna, can you come back please? You were supposed to load the dishwasher, and you've left everything piled up in the kitchen!" yelled Joan.

Knowing full well her aunt had not asked her to load the dishwasher and feeling a wave of dismay at the prospect of being late again, Anna hastily replied, "I'll do it when I get home. I don't want to be late for school!"

"Well that's just too bad. You should have been more organised. You can get yourself back here now please!" Joan retorted.

Amy and Laura sniggered, but before Anna had time to return to the house, Sophie wailed impatiently at her mother.

"Mum, we break up today and it's the school's Christmas party. I can't carry the cakes, sandwiches and presents on my own! I need Anna to help me!"

"Oh, alright! Make sure you make up for this later!" Joan snapped at Anna before retreating into the house.

Feeling relieved, Anna continued to walk to school with the three girls. Unexpectedly, Sophie's hair caught Anna's attention. It looked a different colour.

"Sophie, what have you done to your hair!" Anna exclaimed. "It's got yellow streaky bits in it!"

"I don't know what you mean," said Sophie. "It's the same as ever."

"No, it isn't!" replied Anna. "You've bleached your hair, and it's gone wrong!"

Amy and Laura stared at Sophie's hair, which had uneven patches of lighter shades.

"Look, Anna!", Sophie roared. "I have *NOT* done anything to my hair! I used a shampoo that happened to bring out the natural highlights in my hair. It worked on me because my hair is naturally blonde. It wouldn't work on you because your hair is a dull colour."

Now that Sophie had taken the emphasis off herself, Amy and Laura looked at Anna's hair disapprovingly, despite the fact that Anna's hair was a beautiful shade of golden brown.

"Sophie's right, you know," said Amy.

Anna just sighed and rolled her eyes in disbelief. It was blatant Sophie had tried to lighten her hair and it had gone terribly wrong, yet, because of her confident denial, Amy and Laura went along with it. It reminded Anna of a story her mother had told her years ago about an emperor with no clothes. In the story, there was an emperor who was keen to have a magnificent suit to wear while riding through his town on horseback.

The emperor had commissioned a tailor who promised to make him the best suit in the land. Unable to come up with fine enough material, and fearing recrimination, the tailor decided to trick the emperor. He assured the emperor that he had indeed produced the finest suit in the land, but only those worthy of their position could see the fine piece of clothing.

In reality, there was no suit; it was all a trick! Although the emperor could not see the suit, he did not want to contradict the tailor and appear stupid or unworthy of his lofty position, and so he declared it the finest piece of clothing in the land.

The emperor rode his horse naked through the streets while the crowd commented on the splendour of his new 'suit,' instigated by the tailor who had arranged for town criers to announce the appearance of the king in his 'amazing' new suit.

The moral behind the story was to emphasise the consequences of going along with everyone else for fear of being different or appearing stupid.

The story was certainly reminiscent of Sophie leading her followers with untruths no-one would dare question for fear of seeming like the only one not to believe her.

"Come on," urged Sophie. "We will be late if we don't get a move on. Ignore Anna, she's just jealous." Sophie quickened her pace and as she turned the corner, she slid in the snow, causing her to bump into Mrs Trotter, an elderly neighbour returning from the local shop. Moving quickly, Anna took hold of the old lady's arm and helped her to regain her balance before she fell to the ground.

"You should watch where you're going," snapped Sophie. "I almost dropped my cakes!"

Amy and Laura, despite having the grace to look a little uncomfortable, said nothing in the elderly woman's defence. Anna, shocked at Sophie's callous behaviour, stared angrily at her cousin and shouted:

"It wasn't Mrs Trotter's fault. It was your fault! You're the one who should watch where you're going. I can't believe you did that!"

"Are you alright Mrs Trotter?" Anna asked.

"I'm fine," Mrs Trotter whispered to Anna, a little embarrassed. "No harm done."

Mrs Trotter's soft tone shifted to fierce assertiveness as she turned to Sophie and yelled, "*You*, young lady, should be more careful when you walk around corners, *and* you want to watch your manners!" She then carried on her way, shaking her head as she went.

"Silly old biddy," uttered Sophie, sticking her tongue out once Mrs Trotter's back was turned.

"You can be such a mean idiot sometimes," said Anna.

"And you're just a jealous one," said Sophie, with a snide look on her face. Sophie brushed past Anna to link arms with Amy and Laura. The three girls quickened their pace to leave Anna trailing behind them with the Christmas party bags.

* * * * * *

The morning passed quite quickly. Fortunately for Anna, since she was not flummoxed from being late that morning, she was able to focus on her work. Miss Marmaduke even smiled in approval at Anna when she solved a maths equation which no-one else had done. Ignoring Sophie's scathing looks, Anna carried on with her work. She wasn't looking forward to the Christmas party as she expected to be picked on by Sophie and her friends.

At twelve midday, the class finished for the last time that year. Miss Marmaduke, who wanted to give a speech about how she hoped her students would aim to achieve more in the New Year, gave up trying to talk when the sound of her voice was drowned out by the scraping of chairs and the loud chatter from the children as they hurried to leave the classroom.

Tables in the assembly hall had been pushed together and covered with red tablecloths. Everyone seemed happy, not just because school was breaking up for two weeks, but because Christmas was coming.

The children took their seats, sitting with the people they preferred most, and started to pull crackers. Plates of sandwiches and cakes were laid out on the tables with jugs of orange juice and water. Even the teachers had lapsed into party mode. Keen to take part in the festivities, the teachers were wearing party hats and seemed more than willing to help the canteen staff lay the tables with extra plates of sausage rolls and pastries.

Anna waited to see where Sophie sat and then opted for a different table. As others began to take chairs at her table, Anna felt an uncomfortable feeling wash over her when she realised no-one was sitting next to her. She hadn't even wanted to come to the stupid party. She was just about to leave the table to wait in the library until the party was over when David came and sat next to her.

"I called for you yesterday," David said, raising his voice above the noise in the hall. "Your aunt sent Sophie instead."

"I know… I heard," Anna replied.

"It can't be much fun living…" David began.

"I don't want to talk about it!" Anna snapped, feeling a fleeting wave of embarrassment.

"Okay." David nodded, looking concerned. Suddenly, his face brightened. "I've got you a present. It's in my locker. I'll give it to you after the party."

"Thanks," said Anna, feeling pleased but slightly uncomfortable at the same time. "But I haven't got you anything," she added, subduedly.

"I'll take it back then," said David, pretending to look disappointed.

Anna smiled. Sophie, who was at the other table, caught Anna's eye as she was smiling, and her face turned to stone when she saw that Anna was sat next to David. Sophie then stared at David with an incredulous look on her face. David ignored her and spoke quietly to Anna.

"What's she done to her hair?" he asked. "It looks like it has stripes in it!"

"I don't know what she's done, but she's definitely been messing about with it," said Anna, gazing at her cousin's hair, which now looked streaked with blonde, brown and sage-green tints.

Anna's thoughts were drawn back to the story of the emperor when some of the other children at her table began to speak to her, their friendliness sparked by the realisation that David was showing an interest in her. Marvelling at the predictable outcome of human nature, Anna began to enjoy herself. She found that when she was being accepted she could engage quite amicably and comfortably in conversation. She found that the more relaxed she was, the more others seemed to want to talk to her.

Sophie, meanwhile, was in the throes of telling her friends how many presents she would get for Christmas, "I will probably get more presents from Mum and Dad than last year," she boasted.

"Might you get less now that Anna lives with you?" asked Laura.

"Of course not," Sophie replied. "My parents have plenty of money and they give me everything I want. They're very generous people, and, although it's kind of them to have Anna live with us, they can afford it."

However, Sophie's smug expression disappeared when she noticed David and Anna had left their table. Sophie did not know David had asked Anna to go with him so he could give her the Christmas present he had bought for her.

Anna felt surreal as she followed David out of the hall towards his locker. She could hardly believe he had bought her a present. No-one had shown any interest in her since her parents died. As an only child with no surviving grandparents, she had no one who cared about her, apart from her Uncle Bill of course. However, he couldn't give Anna much attention because he was always busy with work, never mind the demands of Joan and Sophie.

Anna had no other cousins, and the only other extended family member she knew of was an aunt, her mother's sister, who had emigrated to America some years ago with a man who the family had disapproved of. This aunt had not even attended the funeral of Anna's parents after they were killed in the car crash. Nor did she attend the funerals of her own parents, Anna's grandparents, who had died several years ago, within months of each other.

The unusual emptiness and silence in the school corridor added to the surreal feeling of the whole scenario for Anna. For the first time since her parents' accident, Anna felt a small wave of excitement at the prospect of being given a surprise by someone who, it seemed, liked her a lot. As

David handed her a small, heavy object wrapped in Christmas paper, her eyes lit up.

"What is it?" she asked, excitedly.

"Open it when you get home," said David. "I hope you like it. I just wanted you to have something nice that you can hold whenever you feel upset. I know this is the first Christmas without your Mum and Dad... it must be horrible."

"Thanks, David," said Anna. She appreciated not just the present, but his kindness as well. "I'll open it when I get home."

As Anna placed the gift carefully in her school bag, the loud chatter of the other children interrupted the ethereal silence in the corridor as they streamed out of the hall and headed into the cloakrooms, preparing to go home.

"Meet me at the shop by the park tomorrow," said David as his friends called him to join them for a game of football.

"Okay," replied Anna. "I'll see you at eleven."

Anna felt a surge of happiness and, for the first time in ages, felt she had something to look forward to. As Sophie, Amy and Laura approached Anna, she even managed to ignore their insults. It was strange not to recoil from their remarks. They just didn't hurt in the same way now she was feeling happy.

Sophie looked perplexed when she realised her rude remarks were not having the same impact on Anna as before. Realising she was losing her power over Anna, Sophie felt a stab of anger and resentment. She guessed Anna's new-found strength must be something to do with David.

"I think you should know that David feels sorry for you, Anna. Orphan Annie; sad little orphan Annie!" she taunted.

"You know what, Sophie?" said Anna, her blue eyes flashing with anger as she spoke. "You just don't know when to give up. Well, get over it! I'm sorry I have to be in your class, I'm sorry your friend likes me, and I'm even sorrier that I have to live with you!" she exclaimed. Anna's voice became louder as she continued, "one thing is for certain, as soon as I'm sixteen I will be *GONE*! I can't wait to leave your house. You've been vile since the day I came, and I'm counting the days until I can leave!"

"Are you kidding?" shouted Sophie. "I have to wait three whole years to have my house back!" Turning to her friends for affirmation, she added, "see what I have to put up with? She's so *ungrateful*!"

"Don't get upset," Amy said, trying to soothe a fierce looking Sophie. "Come on, we'll walk home with you. Just ignore Anna."

Anna shook her head in disbelief as Laura and Amy linked arms with Sophie and looked resentfully in Anna's direction. Deep in thought about the fact that she no longer felt so alone, Anna paid little attention to their bitter looks. *Well at least I have a good friend now... That is all I need. Just one special friend and it makes everything more bearable.*

CHAPTER THREE

Anna walked home alone from school, and for the first time it didn't bother her that she was on her own. She couldn't wait to get to her bedroom where she could look in private at the gift David had bought for her. Arriving at the house before Sophie, she let herself in with her key and rushed upstairs. After closing her bedroom door behind her, Anna removed the present from her bag.

Anna felt a rush of excitement as she unwrapped the most beautiful snow globe she had ever seen. Inside the globe there was an exquisite angel with long dark hair, silver wings, and a shimmering blue dress. Shaking the snow globe, Anna gasped as a flurry of white and silver shards covered the angel. Staring in admiration at the gorgeous colours, she suddenly saw something so bizarre that she thought she was dreaming. As the dispersing snowflakes and glitter settled, instead of the angel re-emerging, something else had taken her place.

The angel had disappeared and in its place Anna could see an image of an attractive woman in her late thirties with shoulder length golden-brown hair and hazel eyes. The woman was walking down a terracotta paved driveway leading to a small detached house with decorative stained glass windows and a blue front door.

Engrossed by the enchanted scene in front of her, Anna hardly heard her Uncle Bill's voice calling her from downstairs. Anna's eyes momentarily left the snow globe as she directed her attention to her uncle's voice. When she looked again, the woman and the cottage had disappeared. The angel had returned.

Stunned and staring open mouthed in disbelief, Anna shook the snow globe again. This time, after the flurry of white and silver had settled, all that was revealed was the original angel. Hearing Bill call to her again, Anna placed the snow globe in a bag inside the drawer of her bedside table and made her way downstairs.

Anna forgot about the unbelievable snow globe incident for a while as she was brought back to reality upon seeing her Aunt Joan and Sophie sitting with Uncle Bill in the living room. Unlike her bedroom, the living room was warm and inviting with comfortable cream walls and expensive rugs. The newly bought lamps emitted a soft pink light and created a cosy atmosphere. A warm glow shone from the log-effect gas fire, situated in the recently installed white fireplace.

Joan had certainly splashed out lately. Sophie and her mother were watching television and ignored Anna when she entered the room. Bill spoke kindly to her, his blue eyes full of concern.

"How are you Anna? I don't get to see much of you these days, with work and everything else going on. I know this must be a difficult time for you."

"I'm okay," Anna replied. "Did you want me?" she asked, eager to change the subject. For an instant she felt scared that if Uncle Bill showed her any more concern, she might break and burst into tears. She had held back her emotions for so long and her determination not to cry had become a defence mechanism which kept her going.

Although her uncle felt concerned that Anna may be bottling things up, he decided not to push things any further. He didn't want to upset her.

"My work is holding a Christmas party on Saturday and our families are invited to go too. It should be good. They're planning a live band, dancing and there will be plenty to eat. I'd like you all to come. It's at the clubhouse in the park at seven this Saturday evening."

"Yeah, that will be good," replied Anna.

"Who else is going, Bill?" asked Joan.

"All the management team, and most of the twenty-five employees with their families. That also includes Paul and Sue over the road with their lads, Stephen and Callum. Oh, and Pete and Carolyn will be there with their lad, David. David's in your class at school, isn't he?" asked Uncle Bill, addressing Sophie and Anna.

33

"Yes, he is," Anna said with a smile.

Sophie gave Anna a look of contempt and then returned her attention to the television. Joan glared at Anna and left the room, saying she was going to prepare dinner. Bill appeared oblivious to his wife's and daughter's treatment of Anna. He suggested to Anna that she sit down with them to watch television. He was secretly concerned with the fact that she always seemed to be in her room these days.

Despite feeling uncomfortable, Anna sat down on the sofa next to Sophie. Unbeknown to her cousin, Anna was secretly counting the minutes until she could return to her room and hold her precious snow globe.

Joan called from the kitchen for the family to come and sit down for dinner. Anna had no appetite because of her earlier excitement and planned to go straight upstairs to the snow globe as soon as the dining table was cleared.

Once they were seated around the table in the large kitchen, Anna tried to eat as much as she could for fear of offending her aunt. Bill couldn't help notice the way Sophie was scowling at Anna from across the table and wondered what had happened between the girls this time.

"Pleased you've broken up from school, girls?" Bill asked, hoping to change the strained atmosphere around the table.

"Yeah, I love Christmas, Dad," Sophie replied, with a contented look on her face. "I love all the presents, but I love to give as well... I mean that's what it's all about isn't it?" she added, self-righteously.

Anna, amazed at her cousin's falseness, couldn't help mutter under her breath: "More like *taking* in your case!"

"Sorry, Anna, what was that you said?" challenged Sophie, her eyes narrowing.

"Forget it," snapped Anna.

"Really, Anna!" exclaimed Joan, angrily. "It would be nice if you appreciated the fact you have a family to live with. A family willing to take you in when..."

Bill interrupted his wife before she could finish. "Leave it Joan, please," he said, firmly. Then, looking at Anna, he said, "Anna, I know it's hard for you, particularly at this time of year, but I promise it will get easier in time. Just..."

"Oh, for God's sake, Dad!" snapped Sophie, before Bill could finish what he was saying. "Why do you stand up for her so much? Can't you see she's just after attention all the time?"

"Sophie's got a point, Bill," added Joan, trying to keep the anger out of her voice, while Sophie smirked at Anna.

Anna suddenly felt that dizzy feeling again. She thought she would faint. She could hear Sophie and her aunt and uncle's voices, but they seemed distant and fuzzy. She felt she had to escape from the kitchen and get to her room where she would feel safer.

"I wish you'd stop talking about me as if I'm not here! I wish you would just leave me alone!" Anna screamed, as she left the room.

"Well, honestly!" Joan shouted, pretending to be shocked by her niece's outburst. "We have a problem child on our hands. She's such a bad influence on Sophie, Bill. You don't know half of what we have to put up with!"

"Oh, give it a rest, Joan!" Bill exclaimed as he left the table, not taken in by his wife's feigned upset over Anna's outburst.

"That girl causes so much trouble in this house," Joan hissed.

"I know, Mum," said Sophie, with a pained expression on her face. "Do we have to keep her? She even has to come to school with me!"

"The trouble with people like us, Sophie," began her mother, "is that we are caring and decent. Without us, that girl would be in care."

"Well, I think we can be *too* caring and decent," replied Sophie. "Sometimes we should put ourselves first."

Upstairs, Anna lay on her bed and stared at the ceiling, wondering how long she could put up with the cruelty that Sophie and Joan subjected her to. Her dismal thoughts were quickly interrupted when she remembered the snow globe. Feeling a surge of excitement, she got off the bed. Opening her bedside table drawer, Anna carefully removed the beautiful snow globe. Her excitement soon turned to apprehension when she feared she may have only imagined the image of the woman and the house that had materialised in the globe before. She closed her eyes, took a deep breath and gently shook the snow globe.

Praying silently for the miracle to return, Anna opened her eyes. As the snow flurry cleared, she gasped in amazement as a lifelike vision appeared before her. This time it was a different scene to the previous one. Inside the globe was a clear image of a street Anna recognised as Elmtree Way. The image depicted a house with a white door marked with the number twenty-seven in chrome figures.

After a couple of seconds, the image changed to show the inside of the house. It shocked Anna to see Mrs Trotter inside the house, collapsed on the living room floor. In fact, Anna noticed that she wasn't moving at all!

Covering her mouth in horror, Anna trembled, wondering if the old lady was still alive. However, just as before, the image in the globe began to fade and the angel returned. Despite shaking the snow globe vigorously, Anna could not get the image of Mrs Trotter to return. Instantly, Anna realised she had to get to Mrs Trotter straight away. She had no time to marvel at the miracle of the snow globe. She just had to get to Mrs Trotter.

Grabbing her coat, she ran down the stairs without bothering to tell anyone where she was going. Outside, the pavement was slippery as the snow had hardened from the falling temperatures. This did not deter Anna, who ran as fast as she could, despite slipping constantly and having to recover her balance. Before she reached Elmtree Way, Anna almost ran into Stephen, her neighbour, who was delivering newspapers.

"Hey, steady on!" he laughed, as he grabbed Anna to stop her falling over after she almost hurled herself into him. "What's the rush?"

Breathless, Anna replied, "Stephen, I'm glad I've seen you. You deliver a newspaper to Mrs Trotter don't you?"

"Who?" asked Stephen, looking puzzled.

"Mrs Trotter, number twenty-seven, Elmtree Way!" gasped Anna.

"Oh! Oh yeah, I do. I'm just on my way there now," Stephen replied.

"Good, I'll come with you, but we've got to hurry!" shouted Anna, urgently.

"Why?" asked Stephen.

Anna hesitated. She didn't know what to say. She couldn't tell Stephen about the snow globe. Not only was it too nonsensical for anyone to believe, Anna just knew she had to keep it a secret. It might even be dangerous in the wrong hands.

"Um, err," Anna stuttered. "She didn't look very well when I saw her this morning… she was… like, a funny colour…"

"Well, what do you want me to do about it!" retorted Stephen. He was becoming a little uneasy with all the dramatics. "I deliver her newspapers, not her medicine!"

"Oh, forget it!" snapped Anna. "I'll go without you."

"No, it's okay; I'll come with you," Stephen agreed, reluctantly. "I'm going there anyway."

*****

Upon reaching Mrs Trotter's house, Anna pushed open the small gate and walked down the cobbled path that led to a white door. Knocking furiously, Anna began to shout, "Mrs Trotter! Mrs Trotter! Are you okay? Can you open the door?"

Realising this was a waste of time as Mrs Trotter probably couldn't hear her, Anna rushed to the side of the house and tried to open the gate that led to the back of the garden but, to her dismay, she found it was locked.

"Give me a hand up!" she shouted to Stephen. "We've got to get to her somehow."

Ignoring her, Stephen grabbed the top of the gate with both hands, hoisted himself up and jumped over the top of the gate to the other side. Opening the gate for Anna, they rushed around to the back of the house. Looking through the patio doors, they could see Mrs Trotter lying unconscious on the floor.

"Stephen, quick! Call an ambulance!" Anna urged.

Removing his mobile phone from his coat pocket, Stephen called 999 and asked for the ambulance service. Stephen explained that he had been delivering a newspaper to number twenty-seven, Elmtree Way, when he found the owner of the house unconscious on the floor. The operator said an ambulance would be with them as soon as possible.

Although it was only a few minutes, it seemed like ages before Anna and Stephen heard the siren of the approaching ambulance. As the paramedics made their way to the house, Mrs Jenkins, the neighbour from next door, came out asking what was wrong.

Anna told Mrs Jenkins that she had seen Mrs Trotter unconscious on the floor. Luckily, Mrs Jenkins said she had a key to the old lady's house. She also informed the paramedics that Mrs Trotter was diabetic and could be in a coma. After rushing back into her house, Mrs Jenkins returned with a key to Mrs Trotter's front door.

The paramedics were soon at Mrs Trotter's side. Removing a blood sugar count monitor from the medical bag, a paramedic checked Mrs Trotter's sugar level. The monitor displayed an abnormal reading, and the other paramedic adeptly withdrew a syringe from the same bag and administered insulin into Mrs Trotter's arm.

Sliding an oxygen mask over Mrs Trotter's face, the paramedics secured her on a trolley and wheeled her out to the ambulance. As they opened the ambulance doors, Mrs Trotter opened her eyes. Although pale and looking fragile, she was conscious and coherent.

"Who called the ambulance?" she asked, in a weak voice.

"I did," replied Stephen, awkwardly, because he knew if it wasn't for Anna there wouldn't have been an ambulance. "But it was only because Anna was worried about you and made me climb over the gate to see if you were alright."

"Thank you, my dears," answered Mrs Trotter, gratefully. "You probably saved my life."

"Don't you worry about a thing!" Mrs Jenkins told Mrs Trotter before the ambulance doors closed. "I'll take care of the house for you. You just get yourself well. I'll call your children and tell them to go straight to the hospital."

Mrs Trotter smiled and even managed a small wave as the ambulance doors closed. Anna breathed a sigh of relief as the ambulance, with blue light flashing, sped off towards the hospital.

"Thank goodness she's okay!" exclaimed Mrs Jenkins. "Poor Mrs Trotter! It must have been her diabetes. If you kids hadn't acted so quickly, I dread to think what might have happened. A couple of heroes, that's what you are!"

"We only did what anyone else would have done," said Anna, modestly.

Mrs Jenkins turned to look at Anna and Stephen with a puzzled expression on her face.

"How did you know something was wrong in the first place?" she asked, as it dawned on her that there was no logical reason why these two children would have known Mrs Trotter had collapsed.

"Ummmm, just a feeling," replied Anna, feeling uncomfortable.

"Come on Stephen, we'd better go," she added, quickly. "You will be late with the rest of your paper round."

Muttering as polite a goodbye as she could muster, Anna walked away from the probing eyes of Mrs Jenkins while practically dragging Stephen along with her.

"Hang on, Anna!" exclaimed Stephen once they were out of earshot of the curious Mrs Jenkins. "There's no need to pull me. Anyway, how *did* you know something was wrong?"

"I *told* you," she answered, vehemently. "I saw her earlier today and she didn't look too good, and I just had a kind of feeling... that's all! Just a feeling!"

"Look, I have to go," Anna added, impatiently. "Thanks again."

Heading back home, Anna left behind a rather baffled Stephen. He was still trying to work out how on earth Anna could have known Mrs Trotter needed help.

CHAPTER FOUR

Although it had stopped snowing, it was bitterly cold. Anna shivered and pulled her woollen hat firmly over her ears as she made her way to meet David. Her face lit up when she saw him and Benjie waiting for her outside the newsagent.

"Hello, Benjie," Anna said. She stroked Benjie affectionately while he jumped up at her, clearly pleased to see her.

"Hi, you made it then!" David said with a grin, obviously pleased to see her too.

"What do you think I am, some kind of prisoner!" snapped Anna.

"Don't be stupid!" he replied in a light tone. "I was only joking. Come on, let's take Benjie to the park."

Noticing a sports bag on Anna's shoulder, David asked her what was inside.

"David, you will never believe what this is. You won't believe what's happened!" Anna said, excitedly.

"Well go on then, tell me," he replied, raising his eyebrows.

"Wait a minute!" Anna's eyes narrowed as she noticed Sophie and her friends walking towards them.

Sophie approached them with a smile on her face directed at David.

"Hi David." Unable to hide her anger at seeing David with Anna, Sophie's smile disappeared as she stared at her cousin.

"What are you doing with *her*?" Sophie asked David, without taking her eyes off Anna.

Trying to compose herself, Sophie turned her attention back to David, but this time her lips quivered in a nervous smile as she told him she was going to the cinema with Laura and Amy and then asked if he wanted to join them.

"Sophie, I'm with Anna and Benjie," replied David, "and they don't let dogs into the cinema," he added. David was sick and tired of Sophie's constant and pathetic attempts to manipulate him.

"Oh well, you said it," said Sophie, with a sneer as she looked at Anna. "They don't let *dogs* into the cinema, do they!"

Sophie stormed off with Laura and Amy in tow, and David stared after her in disbelief.

"She's *unbelievable*," he said, shaking his head.

"Oh, ignore her," replied Anna, indifferently. "She's pathetic." Touching the bag on her shoulder, she told David she had far more important stuff to think about and urged him to hurry to the park with her.

Angry, David asked how on earth Anna could stand it and how she could carry on living with Sophie and her parents.

Anna, feeling totally hopeless, raised her voice in frustration.

"Because I have no choice! I can't do anything about it so give it a rest will you! Believe me, as soon as I'm old enough I'll be out of there. You just make things worse for me by going on all the time when I can't do anything about it!" She was now on the verge of tears.

"I'm sorry," replied David, soothingly. "I just hate what you have to put up with, that's all. Anyway, what have you got in that bag?" he asked, with an inquisitive glint in his eye.

"Come on, let's go to the park," replied Anna. "I don't want anyone to see."

Looking intrigued, David nodded. They made their way to the small park which was a five-minute walk away.

* * * * *

Reaching the park, David released Benjie from the lead, who followed them happily while they made their way to a bench that overlooked the lake at the back of the local clubhouse.

"Go on then, you can tell me what's been going on!" said David, after making sure there was no-one around as they sat down on the bench.

As David watched, Anna removed the snow globe he had bought her from her shoulder bag. Immediately, David's eager expression changed to disappointment.

"Oh, is that it!" he exclaimed. "I thought you had something really interesting in there."

"I have! It *is!*" replied Anna, excitedly. "David, I'm telling you… this is a miracle!" she exclaimed.

"What do you mean?" asked David.

"Just wait a minute and look," replied Anna. Anna shook the snow globe in front of David, who was now watching intently. Once the flurry of snowflakes had settled and all was clear again, David was staggered to see that the original angel figurine in the globe had disappeared and in its place was an image of Sophie.

"I can see Sophie! I don't believe it... What's happening? It's so weird. I've never seen anything like it in my life! It's incredible!"

Anna, who had become accustomed to the miracle of the snow globe, remained calm as she studied the new scene inside the globe.

"I know! I told you that you wouldn't believe it. The day I took it home I shook it and I saw a lady walking down the driveway to a lovely house. Later, when I shook it again, I saw Mrs Trotter collapsed on the floor in her back room. I took Stephen with me to her house and we called an ambulance. She was in a diabetic coma! Luckily, she's okay now, but if it hadn't been for the snow globe..."

David exchanged an incredulous look with Anna.

"It's unbelievable! Did you say anything to Stephen about it?" asked David.

Anna paled at the thought. "*No*! Don't be daft! David, we can't tell anyone! Don't you understand, if this got in the wrong hands, it could be dangerous. People would know all sorts of things about others and would use the snow globe in a bad way for their own personal gain. Also, it would be worth a *fortune*, and so many people would try to steal it. Can't you see, it must only be used for good!"

"Look!" exclaimed David, who had returned his attention to the scene in the snow globe. The image showed Sophie in her bedroom. She was wailing loudly and calling for her mother while staring at herself in her dressing table mirror. David suddenly noticed something about Sophie and burst out laughing.

"Her hair has gone green! Her hair has gone bright green, and she's hysterical!"

Anna looked into the snow globe and started laughing. Sophie was distraught, becoming even more hysterical and screaming loudly.

"Goodness, what have you done!" screeched Joan. "Your hair! It's gone green! You stupid girl! What have you done?"

"I... I... I've been using a spray to add soft highlights!" spluttered Sophie in between sobs.

"More like bleach spray!" fumed Joan. "If you wanted highlights, I would have taken you to the hairdressers," she added, shaking her head in dismay.

"But the label reads it's supposed to add soft highlights, not turn hair green!" shrieked a tearful Sophie.

By now, Anna and David were laughing uncontrollably.

"Well you've obviously used too much of it!" shouted Joan.

"Mum!" wailed Sophie. "What am I going to do? It's the party at the clubhouse in an hour and I won't be able to go!"

"Well you can't go like that! I'll have to get you a hair dye from the chemist. You won't get time to go to the party, but at least you won't have green hair over Christmas! I'll run over there now to get it before they close."

Joan, clearly annoyed at the stupidity of Sophie and the inconvenience of having to rush to the chemist, banged the bedroom door shut as she left. The scene in the globe began to fade and the angel reappeared.

"Quick, shake it again!" urged David, hardly able to contain his excitement.

Anna shook her head. "It makes no difference. Once the angel comes back, you have to wait until she wants to show you something else. It was the same when I saw the woman and the cottage. It also happened when I saw Mrs Trotter. The one of Sophie and Joan was even more amazing because we could see them *and* hear them!"

"It only seems to show the future," said David. "You didn't recognise the woman walking down her driveway?"

"No, no idea at all. But I know the globe probably showed Mrs Trotter before she had collapsed in real life, otherwise we wouldn't have reached her in time with her sugar levels being so high. Also, the party at the clubhouse is tomorrow, so what we just saw with Sophie must be a day ahead.

"David," Anna continued. "Promise me you won't tell a soul about this. If this snow globe got into the wrong hands, it could cause all sorts of bad things to happen... not just good things. It could give the wrong people the power of knowing the future. People would even kill for this. It has to be our secret and no-one else's."

"I know, Anna. I heard you the first time," replied David, who was beginning to feel irritated by Anna's lack of trust. "I won't tell anyone! What do you take me for?"

"Sorry," mumbled Anna. "I'm just stunned by it all. To be honest though, we don't really know how the angel works. Maybe she only works for certain people but I'm not taking the risk to find out! Where did you buy it from anyway?"

"From the Old Curiosity Shop in town. I saw it in the window and thought you'd like it."

David began to laugh. "I can't believe Sophie's hair! Are you going to warn her about that stuff?"

"No!" declared Anna. "If I tried to tell her, she wouldn't listen anyway because I'm *sooooo jealous of her beautiful hair!*"

David, who had been grinning, suddenly looked more serious. "Let's meet again tomorrow. Bring the globe with you and we'll see if the angel wants us to know about anything else that is going to happen."

"Okay. I'll meet you at the shop again at about eleven," Anna confirmed. "Come on, we'd better get back or I will have my aunt breathing down my neck again."

"Old dragon!" said David, holding Benjie to put on his lead. They left the park together, both wondering what the angel would reveal next.

CHAPTER FIVE

When Anna woke up the following morning, she felt a wave of excitement as she remembered she was meeting David later on that day. She felt even more excited when she thought about the incredible snow globe and immediately retrieved it from the top drawer of her bedside table. Shaking it in anticipation of yet another incredible scene forming before her eyes, she felt mixed emotions of disappointment and relief when nothing changed within the globe. Anna shook it again but the angel remained in place after the initial flurry of white flakes had settled.

Deciding there had been too much drama recently regarding the revelations of the snow globe, she placed it back in the drawer. Instinctively, Anna knew the globe would only reveal significant events that related to *her*. This thought made Anna curious about the first image she had been shown in the snow globe of the attractive woman walking down the pathway of the beautiful cottage. Glancing at the mobile phone her uncle had bought her, she saw a text from David.

DAVID: *Has the globe shown anything else?*

ANNA: *No not yet, we just need to wait and see what happens to Sophie's hair. LOL.*

DAVID: *Can't wait! Meet me at 11.00 a.m.*

Before Anna could reply that she would meet David, she heard Joan calling her name from downstairs.

"Anna, don't get arranging anything today! I've got loads to do and I need your help."

ANNA: *No can do. Joan needs me. Will text later.*

DAVID: *OK. See you at the dance later x*

Anna felt a warm glow when she read David's text and replied, '*OK x.*' She liked adding the kiss at the end of the text.

* * * * *

Despite being piled with chores, Anna thought the day had passed surprisingly quickly. She was reminded of a Nina Simone song her mother had liked called "What A Difference A Day Makes." For the first time, Anna realised what the song actually meant. *"What a difference a day makes… twenty-four little hours… what a difference a day makes… and the difference is you."*

Now Anna understood the whole meaning of the song; *you just need one special friend, and even if you can't see that person as much as you would like, it doesn't matter. Just having that person on your mind makes you feel happier throughout the day and makes everything seem more bearable.*

After wiping down the worktops in the kitchen, Anna glanced at her watch and decided it was time to get ready for the dance at the clubhouse, which would start in an hour and a half. As she made her way up the stairs, she heard Sophie crying to her mother about her hair which had turned green.

Anna laughed inwardly as she recalled the scene from the other day presented to her and David by the snow globe. *Well, the hair disaster has certainly happened*, she thought. As Anna was about to enter her bedroom, Aunt Joan came out of Sophie's room looking annoyed and she eyed Anna coldly.

"You won't be able to go to the dance tonight," Joan said, dismissively.

"Why not?" asked Anna, upset at the thought of not being able to go and see David.

"Because Sophie's not well and she needs someone to stay home and make sure she's alright!" Joan snapped.

"Bill and I are both going, so you must stay here and look after Sophie," she added.

Not wanting to give her aunt the satisfaction of knowing just how upset she was, Anna merely nodded and went into her room. She didn't even bother asking what was wrong with her cousin. She knew it was the green hair and her aunt would never admit to that. Closing the door behind her, Anna lay on the bed and sobbed as quietly as she could. It seemed that any bit of happiness she could muster was snatched away by Joan or Sophie. She wondered how long she could stand for all of this.

* * * * *

Anna must have fallen asleep for over an hour. When she awoke she could hear the television in Sophie's room. She knew Sophie had no intention of getting up after the hair fiasco.

Feeling hungry, Anna went downstairs to the kitchen and fixed herself a sandwich and poured some orange juice. Taking her food and drink into the sitting room, she switched on the television and tried to distract herself.

Although trying to get absorbed in the programme on the television, Anna couldn't concentrate and found her mind drifting to David. She hadn't even checked her mobile phone. No doubt he would have texted her to see why she hadn't turned up. Turning off the television and the lights in the sitting room, Anna took her plate and glass into the kitchen, placed them in the dishwasher and returned to her room.

David hadn't contacted her, so she decided to text him to tell him she wasn't going to the dance.

ANNA: *Can't go because Sophie according to Joan is 'unwell'.*

DAVID: *I might have known*

ANNA: *I'll text you tomorrow. Have a good time.*

DAVID: *Not without you x*

Anna felt a warm inner glow when she read David's text.

ANNA: *See you tomorrow x*

Feeling despondent, Anna reached for the snow globe from her bedside table. Not only was it powerful and protective, it was also beautiful and it was from David. Although she was not expecting the globe to show her anything, she held it tight and shook it gently, enjoying the sense of comfort it gave her. However, as the white flakes cleared, she gasped in amazement. Once again, the angel had disappeared and a different scene was forming in front of her.

As the image became clearer, Anna saw a lake which had frozen into a white sheet of ice. Scrutinising the scene to work out where it was, the image became even more distinct. Anna noticed the clubhouse behind the lake. She looked in horror as she saw a young boy, no more than eight years old, who had started to walk over the frozen lake.

Recognising the boy as Callum, Stephen's younger brother, Anna saw him sliding over the ice as if he were trying to skate. Suddenly, he slipped and fell. The ice below Callum cracked and he fell into the water. He shouted for help but nobody came. *Of course,* Anna thought in dismay, *they would all be in the clubhouse at the dance! Callum must have left the hall unnoticed, and he was alone.*

"Oh no!" she screamed. "Callum will drown!"

Anna needed to think. She had to do something. She couldn't think straight while she was feeling so uptight. Calming herself down with her breathing and relaxation technique, she could think more rationally. She recalled that the globe seemed to depict happenings in the future, but how far in the future was debatable.

The incident with Mrs Trotter must have happened about half an hour after Anna had seen it in the globe. The incident with Sophie's hair actually happened a day later after Anna saw it in the globe. She guessed Callum would be at the dance at this moment so hopefully nothing had happened to him yet. She decided she would call David. He would help Callum. However, when she tried to call David, his mobile phone went to answerphone. His signal must have gone.

Anna had to get to the park straight away! Grabbing her coat from her wardrobe, she ran down the stairs and put her boots on in the hallway.

Not bothering to call up to Sophie to tell her where she was going, Anna left the house and slammed the door behind her. Anna was aware it would take her about fifteen minutes to reach the clubhouse and she prayed she would get there in time.

Racing through the street and trying to keep her balance in the snow, Anna didn't give a second thought to how crazy she must have looked. All she could think of was reaching Callum before he drowned. A thought flashed through her mind as she realised how perceptions changed with situations. The snow had seemed uplifting and pretty a few days ago, yet now it seemed menacing and treacherous.

Although it had taken Anna less than ten minutes to reach the park, it had seemed like an eternity. Breathless and frantic, Anna raced past the clubhouse and headed straight to the lake. As she approached, she could see Callum was just about to set foot on the frozen lake.

"*CALLUM! CALLUM!*" Anna screamed as loud as she could.

There was no response. Callum couldn't hear her because of the loud music coming from the clubhouse. Anna felt as if everything was unreal and time had slowed down. She let out a cry as Callum started to slide across the ice in a skating motion, just like the snow globe had shown her.

Within seconds, she reached the lake and called to Callum, who was now within earshot. To her horror, before he could acknowledge her, the ice gave way and Callum disappeared below into the cold, dark water.

Aware of the dangers of walking or even lying on the ice, Anna instinctively threw herself to the ground by the bank of the lake. She unwrapped her scarf from around her neck. Anna crawled as near as she could to the edge of the frozen lake, which was within a few feet of where Callum had fallen through the ice into the dank, deep water. He was frantically trying to hold on to the edge of the broken ice so he wouldn't get pulled under. Sensing he was on the verge of panic, Anna urged him to keep calm.

"I'm going to throw my scarf to you! I want you to grab it with your free hand. Are you ready?"

Callum tried to nod, his teeth chattering not just from the cold but from sheer terror as well. Anna hurled the scarf towards Callum, but the end landed within a few inches short of his reach.

"Don't move!" Anna screamed, fearful he would throw himself too far forward and break more of the ice. She knew she was at a disadvantage because she was lying flat on her stomach which reduced her ability to throw the scarf far enough. Anna knew she had to make it reach the next time as Callum could disappear under the ice any second.

Praying the scarf would reach, Anna tossed it again using the same swift underarm movement. This time the scarf reached Callum! He grasped it with his right hand.

"As soon as I start to pull you up out of the water, I want you to lie flat on the ice," said Anna, wishing she felt as confident as she was trying to sound.

Callum nodded vehemently, and as Anna pulled him towards her with every bit of strength her body could muster, he felt himself being forced out of the water and onto the ice. Doing as he was told, Callum lay as gently as he could on the frozen lake.

Within a few seconds, Callum was close enough for Anna to grab his hand. However, as she did so, a large piece of ice around Callum cracked and fell into the water. Just as the boy was about to disappear under the ice, Anna managed to reach out and grab hold of his arm, dragging him to the bank of the lake.

For a short while they lay on the bank not speaking or moving. The combination of shock and relief had left them immobilised. Eventually, Anna spoke.

"What on earth were you trying to do out there, Callum?"

"I was bored," admitted Callum, sheepishly. He realised his actions were stupid and he could have drowned. He also realised how much danger he'd put Anna in as she came to his rescue.

"I was bored too," replied Anna. "But I don't walk across frozen lakes and risk drowning myself," she added, adopting a light-hearted tone so as not to embarrass Callum even more. Looking closely at him, she was relieved to see that although he was trembling with cold and shock, he seemed to be breathing effortlessly. Thankfully, he seemed unharmed but she knew he still needed to go to hospital to make sure.

"Look, the main thing is you're safe now, but we need to get you checked. Let's go inside the clubhouse and get your parents."

Before either of them could get up, they heard Paul, Callum's father, frantically shouting his son's name.

"Callum, you're soaking wet!" he roared, seeing Anna and Callum as they scrambled to get up.

"What on earth has happened?" he demanded, with slight panic rising in his voice.

Callum waited for Anna to speak, but before she could reply, his mother, Sue, came out of the clubhouse accompanied by David and his parents, who had heard the shouting outside.

"Callum!" Sue gasped. "We wondered where you were. Are you okay?"

At that moment, Stephen appeared, a look of shock on his face as he took in the state of his brother.

"Callum, what's happened?" he shouted.

"I thought I could slide on the ice," Callum replied with his head down, looking rather shamefaced. "I'm sorry."

"Never mind that!" said his mother, who flung her arms around him. "Are you alright? That's the main thing! Callum, you could have... You could have drowned!"

"I fell through the ice, Mum. Anna saved me. She pulled me out of the water," Callum replied.

David ran to Anna and hugged her fiercely. "You saved Callum's life! Anna, you are so brave!" he exclaimed. "Are you okay?" he asked Anna in a concerned tone.

"I'm fine," Anna replied.

"Anna, I'll go and tell your aunt and uncle," said Callum's mother. "I can never thank you enough for what you have done. You saved Callum from drowning; it was such a brave thing to do!" Hugging her tightly, Sue whispered, "Thank you, Anna, thank you so much my darling."

"It's okay," replied Anna. "Anyone would have done the same."

"Well, that's debatable," said Pete, David's dad. "Here, take my coat," he added, wrapping his overcoat around Anna's trembling shoulders.

"Can we give Anna a lift home, Dad?" David asked his father.

"Yes, of course, but wouldn't you rather go with your aunt and uncle, Anna?"

"Erm, no, not really," replied Anna, unsure of what to say. Anna knew Joan would be livid when she found out Anna had come to the clubhouse after she had been told to stay with Sophie. Anna wasn't in the mood for any confrontation at that moment. She just wanted to get into a warm bath, put on clean pyjamas and get into bed.

"I would really like to go home now if you don't mind," said Anna, keen to just get away from the lake.

Sensing Anna's reluctance to face Joan and Bill, Callum's mother took control.

"Paul, we'll take Callum to hospital and Stephen can come with us," she said, which prompted Pete to suggest to Anna that he take her home.

"Come on, Anna, let's get you home too," said David's father.

Sue thanked Anna again. "Your aunt and uncle will be so proud of you." As Anna turned to acknowledge her, she noticed Stephen was staring at her with a bemused expression on his face that reminded her of how he had looked when the ambulance had taken Mrs Trotter to hospital.

Relieved to get away from Stephen's inquiring stare, Anna made her way to the car park with David and his parents. Anna wanted to be in bed before Joan and Bill returned home to avoid any probing questions she could not answer, particularly in regard to why she left the house to visit the clubhouse.

David's parents insisted Anna sit in the front of the car to have more access to the heater. As Pete drove, David's Mum, Carolyn, touched Anna gently on the shoulder.

"Are you okay, love?"

"Yes, yes, really, I'm fine," replied Anna, softly.

"You were so brave," said Pete, as he pulled up outside Anna's house. "You could have drowned." Looking a little confused, he asked, "How come you weren't at the party earlier? You must have arrived so late."

"I wasn't going to go to the party because Sophie didn't feel well, but... I."

"Dad!" David interrupted, sensing Anna's discomfort. "Leave her alone. She's tired and wants to go to bed."

"Well, lucky for Callum you came when you did," said Carolyn. "Your aunt and uncle are probably on their way home to see you now. Perhaps we should have told them before we brought you home," she added, a little concerned.

"No, I wanted to get back. I was cold," Anna said. "Anyway, Callum's parents probably told them before they left."

David got out of the car and walked Anna to the door. His parents told her they would be round the following day to make sure she was alright.

"Anna, how did you know?" asked David, quietly. "Was it the angel again?"

"Yes. Yes, it was. I'll tell you what happened tomorrow."

"Okay, I'll call you in the morning. Thank goodness you're okay."

"Night," Anna nodded.

"Night." David looked at her earnestly. "I think you're amazing," he said.

Looking pleased by the compliment, Anna opened the front door with her key, which was still in her pocket. Waiting for David to get back in the car, she waved to him and his parents as the car pulled away. Closing the door behind her, she made her way upstairs for the hot bath she had promised herself.

* * * * *

After getting into her pyjamas, Anna went downstairs to the kitchen to get a hot chocolate. As she was going back up the stairs, she heard the key in the lock moments before her aunt and uncle walked into the hallway.

"Anna!" called Bill. "Anna, are you alright? Come down, love, we need to talk to you."

Anna reluctantly went back down the stairs and followed Bill and Joan into the living room.

Switching on the lamps and the fire, Bill insisted Anna sit close to the fireplace to keep warm.

"I couldn't believe it when Callum's mum told us what had happened," Bill said, with tears in his eyes. "Anna, you risked your life to save Callum. Why didn't you come and tell us?"

Before Anna had chance to reply, Joan spoke for her: "Because she's awkward, that's why! She just wanted to show us up in front of our friends to make out we're not supportive. *Going home with David's father*," she added, in a sneering tone. "Making a nuisance of herself and wanting attention, just like she always does!"

"Oh, for God's sake!" exclaimed Bill. "The girl was probably in a state of shock. She would have just wanted to get home. She saved Callum's life, and it was a very brave thing to do!"

"What were you doing there, anyway?" asked Joan, suspiciously. "You should have been at home with Sophie."

Awoken by all the commotion, Sophie appeared in the doorway. Although Anna was still pretty shaken by the episode at the lake and the questions from Bill and Joan, she couldn't help but feel amused as she noticed Sophie's hair was now the colour of cornflakes cereal.

"What's all the noise about?" Sophie asked, sleepily. "What's the drama queen been up to now?" she asked, directing a mocking look at Anna.

Bill was not only disappointed at the callous behaviour of his wife and daughter, he was losing his temper as well. "She saved young Callum's life – that's what she's been up to!" he snapped, feeling a wave of protection towards his niece. "If it wasn't for Anna, he would have drowned. He had fallen through the ice on the lake!"

"Oh, for goodness sake, don't be so dramatic, Bill" Joan retorted. "Callum would no doubt have got off the ice without any help. She probably made the situation worse by going after him in the first place! You know how these kids exaggerate. All she's done is ruin our night!"

By now, Anna had had enough. Drained from the shock of the danger she and Callum had been in, and weary of the constant abuse from her aunt and cousin, she ran out of the room crying. "I don't need this. I can't take any more and I'm going to bed!"

"Anna, don't go!" Bill called after her, despairingly. He knew his attempt to call her back was futile. He understood how she felt and acknowledged that she needed to be on her own.

"Why are you both so awful to the girl?" Bill asked Joan and Sophie, accusingly. "One of these days you'll go too far and I'll be gone!"

"I'm so sick of her causing trouble!" wailed Sophie.

"So am I," agreed Joan, through gritted teeth. As if suddenly becoming aware of her daughter, she cast her eyes critically at Sophie's hair. "Your hair looks *awful*, Sophie! It's different shades of orange and brown!"

"Thanks a lot!" shouted Sophie, in frustration, before she stormed out of the room, leaving her mother shaking her head in exasperation.

CHAPTER SIX

It was nearly a week since the incident with Callum on the lake, and Anna had almost forgotten all about it. If it crossed her mind, a shudder would go through her body that made her feel almost as frozen as she had felt that day on the ice-covered lake when she lay on the cold bank, desperate to save Callum.

The kind counsellor who had spoken with Anna not long after her parents died, had told her how important it was to talk about what happened after a traumatic event occurred. Despite Miss Marmaduke advising Joan that Anna would benefit from counselling after the trauma at the lake, Joan refused by saying that Anna was fine and receiving all the support she needed at home. The whole incident of Anna saving Callum had enraged Joan because it had placed her niece firmly in the limelight. She was determined to make sure Anna would receive no more attention and that included counselling.

Anna had found little time to meet David. Joan always seemed to have a reason to prevent her from leaving the house. Anna managed to meet up with David a couple of times for half an hour when Joan was shopping, but apart from that, they stayed in touch by text.

It was the last weekend before the children returned to school. Anna woke up with a tight knot in her stomach thinking about Sophie and her spiteful friends ganging up on her when they went back to school.

Although it was only about eight o'clock on Saturday morning, Anna could hear the doorbell ringing. No-one was yet up in the house, but whoever was ringing the bell was persistent and was not going to go away. Eventually Anna heard Bill answer the door. She guessed it was probably the postman with a parcel. A minute later, she was surprised to hear Bill excitedly call her name.

"Anna, are you awake?" he shouted up the stairs. "Come down! There's someone who wants to see you!"

Anna quickly put on her jeans and a thick grey sweater, then made her way down the stairs. Standing in the hallway, her uncle was looking at her expectantly. Standing next to him was a stocky, middle-aged man with a round face and kind brown eyes.

Bill introduced the stranger to Anna as Mike Jones, a reporter from the *Wakefield Observer*, their local newspaper.

"Hi, Anna," Mike greeted her, warmly. "A friend of mine was at that party last week and told me about how you saved that boy's life. Callum, wasn't it?"

Bill, enthusiastic about the reporter being in his house, answered before Anna had time to speak. "That's right, she did!" he said, proudly. "This young lady, my niece, saved a young lad from drowning! The ice had broken and Callum, who apparently thought he could skate on the lake, had fallen through. Anna used her quick thinking, common sense and bravery to save him."

"I'd like to run that story, if that's alright with you, Anna?" said Mike, looking at her with admiration.

"I was going to wait until Monday and call you first," he added, apologetically to Bill, "but I would like to take some photographs by the lake while it's still frozen and the ice may have thawed by then."

"Come through into the living room!" Bill gestured the reporter inside. "We can discuss it in there."

As Bill invited Mike to sit down, Joan entered the room.

"What's going on?" she asked. "What's everyone getting so excited about?"

"Good morning," said Mike, a little taken aback by the unfriendly, tight-lipped woman who entered the room. "My name is Mike Jones. I'm a reporter from the *Wakefield Observer*, and I want to run a story on this brave young lady. You must be very proud of her."

"That won't be possible," Joan said, frostily. "We like to keep a low profile in this family, and all it will do is make us feel uncomfortable."

Bill glared at his wife. It dawned on him how badly Anna had been treated by his wife and daughter. He felt a surge of dislike for the woman he had once loved and treasured. Joan had been lovely when they first met but it seemed as if she had focused any dissatisfaction with her life onto Anna, who had in fact, needed the most support.

"I think Anna should be the judge of that," Bill said, coldly.

"No, it's okay, Bill," said Anna, who was now embarrassed by the whole episode. She decided it wasn't worth the hassle, knowing how mad her aunt would be if Anna appeared in the newspaper.

"It's *NOT* okay!" shouted Bill, his eyes narrowing in contempt as he looked at his wife.

Joan had never seen Bill act this way. Suddenly, she felt scared. Bill looked like he despised her. Disconcerted by his reaction, and overwhelmed by her own emotional response, Joan sat down in silence.

Anna, keen to keep the peace, looked anxiously at Bill and then at Mike, the reporter. "But I didn't really do anything," she said, modestly. "I don't know if anyone will even be interested…" her words trailed off.

"Oh, I think they will," Mike replied. "Not only was it an extremely brave thing you did, you saved a life! I think people will be *very* interested, believe me. Can I make a suggestion?"

Mike continued after Anna nodded her head. "Would you come with Callum and me to the lake so I can take a photograph for the newspaper? I've already spoken with Callum and his parents. They're all in agreement."

Anna looked at Bill for approval. He nodded and smiled in agreement while Joan averted her eyes from Anna and ignored her.

"I'll get my coat!" Anna said, experiencing a sudden sense of freedom after realising that Joan, for once, had been weakened and had lost some of her control over Anna.

As if resigned to the fact she had no influence over Anna this time, Joan stared blankly at the floor. Still devastated by the way Bill had looked at her, she wondered if her marriage was over.

Sophie, who had been listening in the hall, stared icily at Anna as she walked past to fetch her coat. Anna ignored her. Just like her mother, it became apparent to Sophie that she was losing her power over Anna too. Anna was becoming less and less bothered by her, and now, to top it all, she was going to be famous. Feeling jealous and out of control, Sophie ran upstairs in frustration and anger.

Mike's black people carrier drove easily over the icy roads. Due to another flurry of snow, and the fact it was early on a Saturday morning, there was little traffic on the road. Bill sat in the front next to Mike. He decided to go along to support Anna. In the back, Callum was sitting in the middle, in between his mother and Anna. Callum's father was sitting behind with Stephen. Callum's parents were feeling protective of their son and had no intention of letting him go near the frozen lake again without them.

* * * * *

Anna felt good just to be out of the house. It was eight days after Christmas day, which had been a strain. They were invited to Callum's parents for Christmas, but Joan had been sullen because Anna was the centre of attention and Joan had obviously regretted accepting the invitation. Sophie, who had felt the same as her mother, had said she had a headache and left the dinner early to go home and lie down.

For Christmas, Callum's mother had bought Anna a beautiful silver guardian angel pendant. "To keep you safe," she had told Anna, as she watched Anna take it out of the white and silver box.

Sophie had grimaced at Sue when she handed Sophie her present: a box of chocolates. Even Stephen, who never bothered about anyone, was fawning over Anna as if she were someone special.

"How rude!" Sophie had later complained to her mother, in a voice loud enough for Anna to hear. "Callum's mum is just taken in by Anna. It's not fair, Mum. I'm generous enough to share my home with her and *she's* getting all the glory."

* * * * *

As Mike pulled up outside the clubhouse, all of his passengers braced themselves for the cold as they left the warm comfort of the car. Walking towards the lake, Sue placed a protective arm around both Callum and Anna.

Once they reached the lake, Sue shuddered as she pondered over what might have happened if Anna hadn't been there to save her son. Sue could see where the ice had broken in the distance, revealing some of the lake's cold and murky water.

As if he knew what Sue was thinking, Mike took control of the situation. "Come on, kids," he said, trying to lift the agitated atmosphere. He had two children himself and knew only too well the frightening thoughts that were probably going through the adults minds.

"Let's get these pictures out of the way, and then how about burgers and chips to warm us up?"

"Sounds like a good idea!" said Bill, with a grin. Callum gave Anna a high five and then they turned their attention towards Mike, who was instructing them where to stand.

"Not too close to the water," he insisted. "Just about here, where I'm standing now," he said, ensuring they would be a safe distance away from the lake. Mike knew everyone must be nervous, and it was important they all felt safe.

"Callum, I want you to point in the distance to the broken ice. Anna, I want you to link arms with Callum."

Mike began to take a succession of photographs, the camera whirring and flashing. After a few minutes, when he had all the pictures he needed, Mike suggested everyone get back in the car and head for the restaurant. Feeling the cold, everyone rushed back into the car. The mood in the car was lighter and far more relaxed than before. Anna noticed that Bill seemed more preoccupied than the other adults and wondered what was bothering him.

When they arrived at the restaurant, Anna felt comforted by its warm atmosphere. She felt bonded by the experience that none of them would ever forget. Anna felt a wave of contentment for the first time since her parents had died. Apart from David, she had felt disconnected from everyone, but now she remembered what it's like to feel like part of a family. Anna remembered what it was like to feel safe, to be herself, and where she felt free to have fun and to laugh without fear of being criticised or ridiculed.

It was a bittersweet moment because it highlighted just how unhappy Anna had been. She knew she had to get away from Joan and Sophie. She knew things would not get better if she stayed in their house. Her feeling of contentment was quickly replaced by a sudden feeling of doom in the pit of her stomach as she realised she was trapped. There was nowhere for her to go. Anna had no choice but to stay with her aunt and cousin, for now.

CHAPTER SEVEN

Three days after the photo shoot, the temperature had risen and the snow began to thaw, changing from a sparkling, crisp white sheet to a dull-grey slush. The noise of the traffic, which had previously been muffled by the thick snowfall, seemed loud and intrusive as people resumed their normal lives by shopping and returning to work.

Joan sent Anna to the shop to get some bread. It was Tuesday, and the new school term would begin the next day. Once again, Anna felt that same feeling of doom in her stomach as she visualised returning to school and all the taunting that would come with it. As Anna entered the shop, she saw Stephen collecting his paper round. He grinned when he saw her and eagerly removed a newspaper from his bag.

"Anna, look! You and Callum are on the front page!" he said, excitedly as he waved the *Wakefield Observer* in front of her. "You're a hero, and now you're famous! Read it!" he urged. "It tells everyone about how brave you are."

Curious about the article, Anna shyly took the newspaper Stephen was offering her. She stared at the photograph of Callum and herself gazing over the lake at the broken ice where Callum had fallen. She read the bold printed headline:

"Girl Risks Her Life To Save Boy From Drowning"

Feeling too self-conscious to read any more, Anna handed the newspaper back to Stephen.

"It wasn't a big deal," she uttered, genuinely.

"That's another thing the article says about you," Stephen retorted. "That you're modest! Anyway, gotta go! I'm late now. Catch you later."

Before Anna had time to say goodbye to Stephen, or even choose a loaf of bread, other people in the shop started to congratulate her.

"You are SO brave!" said a woman with two young children squabbling over a packet of sweets. "That boy's mother will be grateful to you for the rest of her life!"

"This world needs more people like you!" said a man who had stopped to buy a newspaper on his way to work.

The shopkeeper, who was renowned for being miserable, refused payment when Anna offered to pay for the loaf of bread she had picked. He even handed Anna a bar of chocolate.

"This one's on me," he said, with an approving smile. "Only once, mind," he added, teasingly.

Anna felt overwhelmed. She thought she had done what anyone would have done, yet it seemed like everyone felt she was a hero. After thanking the shopkeeper, Anna made her way back home.

Upon returning home, Anna felt proud and happy. She found Joan in the kitchen and handed the bread to her. Anna still had the money for the loaf in her hand until Joan snatched it off her. She knew how everyone felt about Anna. Joan's telephone had rang three times already that morning with friends *complimenting* her on having such a wonderful niece.

"Don't get too big for your boots," Joan said, in a disapproving tone. "People will soon forget about you… and don't make any plans for today; I need you to wait in for a parcel delivery. Sophie and I are going out."

Although Anna had planned to meet David, it didn't really matter. She would invite him over to the house instead. Hopefully he would be gone by the time Joan and Sophie got back.

For a moment, Joan saw the indifference in Anna's demeanour and realised, once again, that she was losing her control over her niece. Despite Joan's efforts to put Anna down and not allow her to outshine Sophie, the opposite had happened. She also knew Anna was deriving a lot of new-found self-esteem from others, and it angered Joan.

Still perturbed by the disapproving way Bill looked at her lately, Joan decided she would have to be more careful and not let her resentment towards Anna be obvious to others. Ignoring Anna, Joan walked past her and called for Sophie to get ready to go into town. Joan was even more livid when she heard Anna hum cheerfully as she put the kettle on to make a drink. *That girl's getting too thick a skin*, Joan thought, her face taut with anger.

CHAPTER EIGHT

The return to school was dismal for Anna, but there were some bright moments during break times when she was able to hang out with David. It was so much better having someone to be with instead of scouting around for someone to attach herself to in order to avoid the engulfing self-conscious feelings of being alone and rejected.

When Anna was with David, Sophie and her friends didn't bother to bully her. It was a welcome relief to avoid the snide remarks and sneering looks which made Anna's stomach lurch, forming a physical pain that was later replaced by a feeling of emptiness. Sometimes she felt as if there was a great void inside of her. At least during the lunch hour Anna could go into the canteen and get something to eat, something she had avoided since she had joined the school in the previous spring.

"Anything happen with the globe?" asked David, as he bit into his apple.

Anna shook her head. "No, I've shaken it a few times, but nothing. It only seems to show us something when someone needs help or if something important is about to happen."

She thought back to the first image the globe had shown her of the woman and the house with the blue door, but she still couldn't link it to anyone she knew. "Maybe it's just stopped working, I really don't know."

"Well, it's an awesome thing," replied David. "Just awesome! And it only seems to work for something good. There doesn't seem to be anything bad about it even though it's obviously some kind of magic."

"I don't see it as magic," said Anna. "I see it as an angel sending a message."

"Or maybe someone from Heaven?" David asked, gently.

Anna's eyes filled with tears, but this time the tears were comforting and didn't sting. "Maybe," she said, softly.

* * * * *

Arriving home after school, Anna noticed a red car parked outside the house. Thinking nothing of it, she put her key in the door but before she could turn it, Bill opened the door. His face was beaming as if he had something good to tell her.

"Anna, come in, there's someone I want you to see," he said, warmly. Following her uncle to the living room, Anna saw an attractive woman in her late thirties with shoulder length golden-brown hair and a kind face. She was sitting on the sofa. Letting out a gasp, Anna realised it was the same woman she had first seen in the snow globe – an image which had made no sense to her until now. *But who was she? Why did the globe show her to me? Why is she here?*

The woman looked at Anna and stood up. In a gentle voice she said, "Hello, Anna. I'm Clara, your mother's sister."

Anna stared in stunned silence as the woman continued:

"I left for America years ago after a family row. Your grandparents didn't approve of the man I wanted to marry. For the first few years in America, I was too stupid and stubborn to contact them. They were right about my husband but, by the time we had divorced, I never had the courage to contact them again. I was so scared they wouldn't forgive me… I couldn't face them."

"I've heard of you," Anna said. "Mum told me she hadn't seen you in years because of a family row or something."

"I wish I hadn't been so headstrong," said Clara. "I returned to England three months ago, and when I tried to trace them I learned that not only had my parents died a few years ago, but your Mum and Dad had died in an accident. I'm so sorry, Anna. You have lost both of your parents and you must miss them so much."

Anna nodded. "I do miss them," she said, wistfully.

"I can't believe they're all dead," said Clara. "And to think I didn't even attend one funeral. I can never forgive myself for that."

"It's not your fault," said Bill, kindly. "Your sister often blamed your parents for the way they handled things. You were young and in love. Your sister always said they should have been more understanding."

"Thanks for that, Bill," Clara replied, gratefully. "But I still blame myself. At least I have surviving family though... the only family member I have left," she said, looking appreciatively at Anna. "You are the image of your mother, you know."

Clara turned her attention to Bill. "I'm sorry, Bill. I have to remember you lost your brother in that accident. It must be hard for you too."

"I'm coping," replied Bill. "I'm coming to terms with things and accept them. The main thing now is that you and Anna have each other, and I think that is so important."

"That's one reason I'm here," replied Clara. "I returned from the States not even knowing Anna had been born."

Clara continued to explain how she had contacted a local solicitor who, she recalled, had done some legal work for Anna's grandparents when they had moved to a new house years ago.

"When they told me my parents had died I was devastated, but when they told me about Cherie and James and the car accident, the shock was even greater. They were both so young, and it was so tragic." She turned to Anna, struggling to hold back the tears as she spoke. "I really believed I had lost all of my surviving family members until Jane, the solicitor, told me my sister had a daughter. I was going to try to find you, but the newspaper did it for me!" she said, in amazement.

Anna listened intently, her eyes darting from side to side as if trying to make sense of it all. Although overwhelmed, she felt a deep sense of relief that her mother's sister was here with her.

"What you did, Anna, was incredible," said Clara, softly. "I knew it was you when I saw your photograph, not just because of the name but because you're the spitting image of Cherie, your Mum."

Clara turned her attention to Joan, who had just entered the room, but thought twice about extending a warm introduction when she noticed the angry look on Joan's face.

Clara noticed a young girl follow the angry looking woman into the room. Clara thought this girl, who must be Anna's cousin, was nothing like Anna. The girl was tight-lipped and sulky, with a frown on her face that made her look miserable and quite plain.

"Who are you?" enquired Joan. She tried to sound light hearted but she couldn't hide the strain on her face and the nervous tremor in her voice.

Bill spoke for her. "This is Clara, Anna's aunt. Isn't it wonderful that she's come back? She wants to be with Anna."

Joan's reaction surprised everyone, even Sophie. "I thought as much!" she snapped. "After all these years. Why, you've got a nerve! I know your sort," she added, her lip curling in contempt. "You come back when someone is dead to see what you can get!"

Clara gasped in anger. "The only *claim* I want is Anna," she replied, firmly.

"Well you're not having her," retorted Joan. "If anyone thinks that measly allowance I've had from the insurance company is compensation for what I've had to put up with from this brat, then they're wrong. There's a lump sum due on her sixteenth birthday and I'm entitled to oversee it as her guardian."

Bill looked at his wife in horror.

"Firstly, you are *NOT* her legal guardian!" he shouted. "Nothing has been arranged through the courts. Secondly, you are *NOT* entitled to anything of Anna's, and if you have been keeping any of that money she receives, then that is *STEALING!*"

Joan went white with shock. "No, it isn't stealing!" she said, defensively. "I needed it for expenses."

"What expenses?" roared Bill. "I pay all the bills, and Anna hardly has anything. I wondered where you were getting the money from for all the new stuff you've been buying for the house. You've been using Anna's money! I trusted you to withdraw that money to give her an allowance and place the rest in a savings account for her!"

Clara's eyes widened in disbelief. "It's a good thing I came when I did," she muttered to herself. "Anna, I want you to pack a bag and come home with me now. You can't stay with this awful woman a minute longer."

Feeling scared and worried about what people would think if they found out what she had done, Joan turned to Anna and made a futile effort at enticing her to stay.

"I've given you a good home for all these months and looked after you. Be sensible and stay where you belong. We can sort your money out and you can even withdraw it yourself each month. You can do what you like with it!" Joan added, desperately.

"That's not fair, Mum!" wailed Sophie. "What about me having something?"

"OH, SHUT UP, SOPHIE!" Joan yelled at her daughter. "If it hadn't been for you being so jealous of Anna and making my life a misery, things might have been different!"

"Don't blame *me* because *you're* in the wrong!" retorted Sophie, who refused to take criticism from anyone.

Bill stared at his wife and daughter in disbelief. "I can't believe what you've turned into after all these years," he said to Joan, in a trembling voice. "As for *you*, Sophie, you are turning into your mother! You are nasty and selfish. I'm ashamed of both of you!"

Joan called after him as he stormed out of the room. "Bill, where are you going?"

"I'm going to pack a case too," he replied. "I'm leaving, Joan. I will book into a hotel until I find my own accommodation. I'll let you have a forwarding address when I get it."

Returning to the room for a few seconds, Bill spoke to Anna in a low voice. "Anna, do as Clara says. Go and pack a bag and leave with her. Clara can give me her address and I will contact you soon. You'll be much happier with Clara, love."

Anna nodded gratefully and went upstairs to pack.

Joan was now looking frantic and scared.

"Bill, please don't go! You know you don't mean it. We can't manage without you! Stay and we can sort this mess out. It's not as bad as it seems."

"Actually, it's worse," said Bill, coldly. "I should have seen the truth about how you were treating Anna earlier but I ignored it, hoping things would change. Well, they haven't and I'm going. We're *both* going," he emphasised. "I will contact you when I have a forwarding address."

Joan and Sophie were both in shock. There was nothing more Joan could say. Bill and Anna were leaving. Looking at Bill, Clara felt a surge of pity for the man who had not only lost his brother but had now lost his marriage. She handed him a card with her address on it.

"Call soon," she said to Bill. "Come and see Anna any time. She will be in good hands, I promise."

"I know," replied Bill, before he went upstairs to pack.

Clara headed to the car to wait for Anna.

"What do we do now, Mum?" asked Sophie, who was beginning to feel sick.

"Nothing," Joan replied, bitterly. "Your father will be back when he comes to his senses. I knew that girl would be trouble from the start."

CHAPTER NINE

"I'm sure you will like the house," Clara told Anna as they drove away. "It's only about twenty minutes from here, and it's really lovely."

"I think I know what the house looks like," said Anna. "Is it a house with decorative stained glass windows, a red driveway and a blue door?"

"How on earth did you know that?"

"Clara, it's a long story, and it may seem far-fetched. It's to do with a snow globe with an angel inside. You may not even believe me and I don't blame you if you don't, but I promise I'll tell you when we get there," replied Anna, earnestly.

"I'm fascinated," said Clara, smiling. "Can't wait to hear it."

Anna chatted with Clara about her parents for the rest of the drive. It was good to have someone to talk to about them, an older person who understood. Secretly, Anna was worrying about whether she should have told Clara about the globe. After all, she had only just met her, and she had made David promise not to tell anyone. Now she had told Clara. *What if Clara thinks I'm a liar or a crazy person? Who could blame her? What if she does believe me and tells others about the globe?*

The questions nagged at the back of Anna's mind for the whole journey. Maybe she shouldn't have said anything. Trying to rationalise it, she told herself that David had believed her and he would vouch for the globe if necessary. He had seen what happened when Sophie's hair turned green. Also, deep down she felt she could trust Clara, and the snow globe wouldn't have shown such a lovely image of Clara if she was the sort to let Anna down... surely the angel would have warned her.

Realising her anxiety was allowing her thoughts to get out of control, Anna started her breathing exercises and relaxed her body. She began to calm down, and her thoughts became less worrying.

When they pulled up outside Clara's house, it was exactly like the one the angel had shown Anna in the snow globe. Anna felt a sudden burst of exhilaration as she realised how fortunate she was to be the holder of something so powerful and extraordinary. It really was a gift from Heaven, and it made her feel special and warm inside, particularly now she was away from the gloom she had felt in her aunt's house. Anna now had the start of a new life and she was so grateful.

Once they were inside the house, Clara showed Anna to her bedroom. It was delightful. Lilac and cream blinds hung in the window which overlooked a pretty garden and a blue summer house. The walls were painted cream, and Clara suggested Anna could choose her own colour scheme and they could re-decorate the room together, if she wanted. The double bed, covered by a lilac and cream duvet that perfectly matched the blinds, looked inviting. The room was also carpeted in cream, adding a feeling of luxury to the space.

"I rented the house when I first came back from the States," explained Clara, "but I'm now in the process of buying it, so it will be our own home."

"I don't know what to say," whispered Anna. "Thank you."

"You don't have to say anything," laughed Clara. "You are my niece, and as far as I'm concerned, this is your home as much as it is mine."

As Anna looked at Clara and noticed the genuineness in her hazel eyes, Anna knew she could trust Clara with her snow globe secret.

"Let's go down and chat," offered Clara. "You can sit in the kitchen while I make us something to eat. I don't know about you, but I'm starving!"

"I'll tell you about the snow globe," said Anna.

＊ ＊ ＊ ＊ ＊

Anna sat at the oak kitchen table while Clara prepared a cheese omelette. Placing the snow globe on the table, Anna invited Clara to hold it.

"It's beautiful," said Clara, admiringly.

"It has powers," said Anna, almost reverently. "When something important is going to happen, the angel shows it in the globe. It's like watching a movie!"

Anna continued to tell Clara everything that had happened from the time the globe showed her the image of Clara and the house. Clara listened intently without saying a word. However, she laughed when she heard about Sophie and the green hair. When Anna became quite emotional as she talked about the experience at the lake, Clara took her hand.

"Anna, you are so brave. You could have been dragged in and drowned."

"I know, but I didn't think of that until after. I just knew I had to get to Callum," Anna replied.

When Anna had finished her story, she looked at Clara, pleadingly. "You do believe me, don't you? You don't think I'm crazy or making it up?"

"No, of course not!" Clara replied, vehemently. "I believe that sometimes, when we are in need, we get messages to help us. Of course I believe you."

Relieved, Anna thanked her.

"I would like to meet David," said Clara. "You will have to invite him over."

"That would be great," said Anna. "The only thing that's worrying me…" Anna's words drifted off as she turned her attention to the snow globe.

"What is it? What's wrong?"

"The angel has stopped working. When I shake the globe, nothing happens, nothing else appears."

Clara looked at Anna. "Anna, it's most likely that the angel only works when someone is going through a terrible time and needs help. Perhaps… perhaps it's time to let her go and help someone else," she said, gently. "There may be a person out there who really needs her at this moment."

"Of course! Of course!" said Anna, the truth dawning on her. "That explains it! Why didn't I think of it? It was selfish of me to think I might be the only person in the world to need her and that she was only meant for me. What shall I do?"

"Well, as David bought it for you, and the angel obviously trusted him to see how she worked, maybe you should talk to him first. Where did he get the globe from in the first place?"

"The Old Curiosity Shop in Gate Lane," said Anna, quietly. "Do you think we should take it back?"

"Speak to David," said Clara. "I'm sure you'll come up with the right decision together."

Anna nodded in agreement. "I will. I'll call him later."

CHAPTER TEN

Anna invited David to the house the following Saturday. When she went to open the door, Anna was surprised to see Bill with him.

"Bill, what a surprise!" she exclaimed, as she hugged him. She smiled at David as he explained that he had been standing at the bus stop on his way to see Anna when Bill had driven past and offered him a lift.

"Come in, both of you," said Clara, who had joined Anna in the hall. "Lovely to see you, Bill. Good to meet you, David." She was pleased to see them both.

"Hi," said David. "It's good to meet you too."

"Anna, why don't you take David into the kitchen and make a drink?" suggested Clara.

"Okay," said Anna, cheerfully. "You and Bill go and sit down. I'll make you a coffee."

"Nice lad," said Clara, commenting on David as she took Bill through to the living room.

"He has been so good for Anna," said Bill.

In the kitchen, David sat down at the table while Anna made coffee and poured some Coke for David and herself.

"I like your new home," said David. "I'm so glad Clara came for you. Can you imagine if…"

"Don't!" Anna shuddered at the thought of still being at the mercy of Joan and Sophie. "I'm moving school too, so I won't have to bother with Sophie or her cronies."

"Lucky you," said David, rolling his eyes.

"David, I want to talk to you about something."

"Go on then, shoot. What's the problem?" David knew from Anna's tone she was serious.

"It's about the snow globe," she began, as she handed him his drink. "It has to go back. I was talking to Clara about it and…"

"Anna!" he retorted. "You said yourself we shouldn't tell anyone! Not a living soul!"

"I know! I know, and I'm sorry, but I trust Clara and I had to share it with her. She won't tell anyone; she knows it would be wrong if she did."

"Well why does it have to go back? I don't understand… I bought it for you as a present and it's so amazing. Why would you want to give it up? You also said we must never let it get into the hands of anyone else or it could be dangerous!"

"I know I did, but I was wrong!" Anna exclaimed. "After speaking with Clara, I realised I had to have trust in something so good. David, the angel's work is based on good. I don't believe the angel would work for someone if the globe was in the wrong hands."

"How do you know it won't work for you again? Have you tried?" asked David.

"Yes! Of course I've tried!" said Anna, exasperated. "Loads of times and nothing happened! I know deep down that the angel was meant to come to me and has now served her purpose. She needs to move on and help someone else."

As if resigning himself to the fact Anna was right, David sighed and agreed.

"Okay, you're probably right. We'll take it back to the shop. When should we go?"

"Today. I'll ask Bill to give us a lift into town. Help me with this coffee, please."

CHAPTER ELEVEN

"Anna, I've got something I want to talk to you about," said Bill, as he took a sip of his coffee.

"Sit down, both of you," said Clara, letting David know he was welcome to stay and listen.

Bill took a deep breath and continued. "I've decided to go back to Joan and Sophie. I know they gave you a terrible time, Anna, and it's unforgivable, but they've promised me they've changed."

Anna wasn't so sure, but she was pleased Bill and Joan weren't splitting up over her.

"Sophie wants you to have this," Bill said. He handed Anna an envelope. "I don't know how you feel about accepting it – it's an apology. Sophie said she would understand if you didn't want to read it, but she hopes you will."

Clara looked concerned and David looked annoyed, but neither said anything. They both knew it was Anna's decision whether to read the note.

"Sophie told me she realises how selfish she's been," Bill continued.

"She admitted she was jealous of you and worried everyone would prefer you over her. It seems she has very low self-esteem. It was something I should have picked up on, but I've been so busy with work lately. I suppose I've neglected everyone, really."

"Don't blame yourself, Bill," said Anna, with a concerned frown on her face.

"I'm partly to blame, Anna. I've been distant from Joan for some time and I've made her unhappy. I know it's no excuse for the way they've treated you, but I want you to know they haven't always been like that. It was as if the more unhappy Joan became, the more insecure Sophie got, and I guess they both took their feelings out on you," continued Bill.

Taking the letter out of the envelope, Anna read it slowly.

Dear Anna,

I don't really know how to start, but the main thing I want to say is how sorry I am for the awful way I treated you when you were living with us. You must have felt terrible losing your parents. I know how bad I felt when Dad left, so to lose both of your parents forever must be awful. In a way, I'm glad Dad left because not only did it serve me right, it made me realise just how horrible I've been to you.

I admit I was jealous of you, and when I started to be nasty, I began to hate myself. It was as if the more I hated myself, the nastier it made me. I just couldn't seem to stop.

I only hope that you are happy now and that things will work out for you. I don't expect you to want to see me again, but if you ever did, I could always come and meet you anywhere you wanted. I promise I will never be awful again, and I hope that one day you can forgive me and we can be friends like cousins should be.

Love,

Sophie

Saying nothing, Anna placed the note back in the envelope and looked at Bill.

"Anna, I'm not excusing either of them, but I know Sophie is so ashamed and is finding it difficult to forgive herself. She said she hates herself even more than she did before. As for Joan, she was devastated when I left, and she too is finding it difficult to forgive herself. Knowing how insecure and unhappy Sophie was made her overprotective. She said it seemed to turn her into some kind of monster."

"What about the money she took from Anna?" asked Clara, who wasn't convinced they had changed.

"She's put every penny back," said Bill, feeling shameful that his wife could be so mean and deceitful. "She said she wants to make it up to you, Anna, and she would really like to see you if ever you're ready. It's your decision though, Anna, and she knows you probably won't want to see her again. She knows you must hate her."

Anna looked intently at Bill. "Bill, I am so happy now, I don't hate anyone. If I decide to see Joan and Sophie, it won't be for a bit."

Anna looked at David, who merely shrugged his shoulders. As far as he was concerned, they shouldn't be forgiven for the way they had treated Anna. However, Anna had experienced enough unhappiness in her young life and she knew that bearing any resentment would be equivalent to hanging on to the painful past.

"I will see Joan and Sophie," she continued, "but not just yet. Maybe in a couple of weeks or so, but I don't ever want to live with them again."

"Of course not," said Bill. "I wouldn't expect you to after the way they have treated you. Also, you're with Clara now. I just wanted you to know the truth. They are both really sorry."

Anna smiled. "Okay Bill. At least I know. I'll tell you when I'm ready to see them."

CHAPTER TWELVE

It was raining when Bill dropped Anna and David off in town. Promising to visit Anna soon, Bill drove home to tell Joan and Sophie the outcome of his discussion with Anna. Although he loved his wife and daughter, he knew they were both weak and would never have the courage and integrity that Anna had. He did know, however, that they were both deeply ashamed and genuinely upset at their callous behaviour. He also knew that although he would find it difficult to forget or forgive what they had done, Joan and Sophie would find it equally difficult to forgive themselves too.

Anna had the snow globe in her shoulder bag. Wet and cold, David and Anna quickened their pace to make their way to Gate Lane. The Old Curiosity Shop resembled its name. The shop was indeed an old building with Georgian-dimpled windows and an assortment of oddments and jewellery on display.

A doorbell rang loudly as they entered, and an old man appeared behind the counter asking if he could help them.

"I bought this from you just before Christmas and we'd like to return it," said David.

"I'm sorry, young man, but I don't give refunds."

"Oh, we don't want anything for it," said Anna. "We just want to give it back."

"Oh, well if that's the case, I suppose I could give you a little something for it, though it will be less than you paid."

"No, it's okay," said David. "We don't want anything. We just don't want the snow globe any more so we've brought it back. Look, I'll put it back here in the window in the same place where I first saw it."

Carefully, David placed the snow globe in the window, mumbled a quick goodbye, and then he and Anna hurried out of the shop, leaving the old man with a rather surprised look on his face.

* * * * *

Two hours after Anna and David left the shop, a girl, aged about fourteen with long dark curls and sapphire blue eyes, stopped to look in the shop window at the snow globe. As if drawn to it, she knew she had to have it.

"Can I help you, young lady?" asked the elderly shopkeeper.

"Can I see the snow globe that's in the window, please?" The girl's voice was earnest, and she had a sense of sadness about her.

Removing the snow globe from the window where David had placed it earlier, the man handed it to the girl. She asked him how much it was.

Looking at it quizzically as if unsure, the man replied, "Well, let me see…
I would say five pounds should do it."

The girl looked crestfallen. She didn't have enough money to pay for the
snow globe. Feeling sorry for her, the old man asked her how much she
was expecting to pay for it.

"Three pounds?" she suggested, hopefully.

The old man rarely gave discounts, yet there was something in the girl's
face that touched his heart, and after all, the snow globe had been
returned at no extra cost to him.

"It's a deal," he said, feeling pleased when he saw the girl's face light up.
"I'll wrap it for you."

37171291R00063

Printed in Poland
by Amazon Fulfillment
Poland Sp. z o.o., Wrocław